PRESSURE *to* PURPOSE

ANSWERS 4 LIFE

30 Day Devotional

DERVON DUNAGAN

XULON PRESS

Xulon Press
2301 Lucien Way #415
Maitland, FL 32751
407.339.4217
www.xulonpress.com

© 2022 by DERVON DUNAGAN

All rights reserved solely by the author. The author guarantees all contents are original and do not infringe upon the legal rights of any other person or work. No part of this book may be reproduced in any form without the permission of the author.

Due to the changing nature of the Internet, if there are any web addresses, links, or URLs included in this manuscript, these may have been altered and may no longer be accessible. The views and opinions shared in this book belong solely to the author and do not necessarily reflect those of the publisher. The publisher therefore disclaims responsibility for the views or opinions expressed within the work.

Unless otherwise indicated, Scripture quotations taken from the King James Version (KJV) – *public domain.*

Scripture quotations taken from the New American Standard Bible (NASB). Copyright © 1960, 1962, 1963, 1968, 1971, 1972, 1973, 1975, 1977, 1995 by The Lockman Foundation. Used by permission. All rights reserved.

Scripture quotations taken from the Contemporary English Version (CEV). Copyright © 1995 American Bible Society. Used by permission. All rights reserved.

Scripture quotations taken from the Gods Word Translation copyright ©1995 by Baker Publishing Group.

Scripture quotations taken from the Good News Translation (GNT). Copyright © 1992 American Bible Society. Used by permission. All rights reserved.

Scripture quotations taken from the New King James Version (NKJV). Copyright © 1982 by Thomas Nelson, Inc. Used by permission. All rights reserved.

Scripture quotations taken from the Holy Bible, New International Version (NIV). Copyright © 1973, 1978, 1984, 2011 by Biblica, Inc.™. Used by permission. All rights reserved.

Scripture quotations taken from the Holy Bible, New Living Translation (NLT). Copyright © 1996, 2004, 2007 by Tyndale House Foundation. Used by permission of Tyndale House Publishers, Inc.

Paperback ISBN-13: 978-1-6628-4514-7
Hardcover ISBN-13: 978-1-6628-4515-4
Ebook: ISBN-13: 978-1-6628-4516-1

TABLE OF CONTENTS

Introduction – Pandemic 2020 v

Week 1 – The Challenges of Life: God Hears Your Prayers 1
    Day 1: Do Not Worry About Tomorrow. 4
    Day 2: Give All Your Worries and Cares to God 7
    Day 3: God Will Rescue You from All Your Troubles. 9
    Day 4: God Will Not Abandon You 12
    Day 5: God Knows Your Needs. 16
    Day 6: The Lord Delights in Answering Prayers. 20
    Day 7: My Journal. 24

Week 2 – What Is the Difference between Knowledge of God's Word and Understanding God's Word? 25
    Day 1: Understanding God's Word 32
    Day 2: Desire, Listen, Understand. 34
    Day 3: Seek Wisdom. 36
    Day 4: Set Knowledge in Motion .39
    Day 5: Understand the Fullness and Purpose for Life. 42
    Day 6: Becoming a Servant of the Lord 46
    Day 7: My Journal. 50

Week 3 – Intimacy and the Mountain...........51
Day 1: Mountain Top Moments...........53
Day 2: Continue Climbing...........55
Day 3: Heart to Heart...........57
Day 4: Learn to Know Him...........60
Day 5: Mountain Moving Faith...........64
Day 6: Intentional Commitment...........66
Day 7: My Journal...........68

Week 4 – Bread Is Necessary...........69
Day 1: God Provides...........71
Day 2: Needs Not Greeds...........75
Day 3: Come! Partake!...........78
Day 4: The True Bread of God Is All You Need...........81
Day 5: Jesus Will Fill Your Emptiness...........83
Day 6: Jesus Is the Answer 4 Life...........88
Day 7: My Journal...........90
Day 29: Conclusion...........91
Day 30: Your Summary...........92
Invitation...........93

A Note from the Author...........94

About the Author...........95

Introduction
PANDEMIC 2020

Midway through February 2020 is forever etched in my memory. It was the beginning of the worst pandemic in two generations. The swift-moving coronavirus began its assault, wreaking havoc on mankind. It took lives faster than we could count, pushed hospitals beyond capacity, forced school closures, business shutdowns, millions of jobs lost, churches required to close their doors, and mandatory "Stay At Home" orders.

The death toll and coronavirus cases climbing at an alarming rate caused chaos, fear, and depression to set in. Online and phone prayer requests were at an all-time high. On March 16, 2020, the Dow Jones plunged 13 percent, 2,997 points. The financial markets were in a free fall. The United States and the world were rocked to its core.

While the world health organization, the CDC (Center for Disease Control), government officials, and local officials searched for answers, another alarm sounded. Americans needed access to the necessities of life. Certain businesses were deemed "essential," such as supermarkets, gas stations, pharmacies, U S Postal service, FedEx, UPS, and Amazon to meet these needs.

I clearly remember walking down the board game aisle at Walmart. I couldn't believe my eyes. The shelves were half empty! We continued on to the fabric and craft section and again my jaw dropped. These aisles were about 25 percent stocked.

On another day, my wife and I stopped in Home Depot, and the line to enter wrapped around the building. As we waited in line, we observed customers exiting with flatbed carts loaded with wood, building materials, paints, and project kits, etc. Once again my jaw hit the ground.

Americans were trying to adjust to a new way of life, which was really an old way of life dating back to the 1950s. Families were home doing life **together**, playing games, singing songs, working on home projects, and enjoying dinner **together** just like the good old days the Lord delighted in.

Ask Yourself…

Has America slowly placed God on the back burner in our schools and our homes?

What happened to prayer in classrooms and the pledge of allegiance being led by teachers as part of the daily agenda?

Are couples no longer placing Jesus at the center of the marriage?

Is Jesus pleased that marriage in America has lost its honor as couples chose to live together instead of marriage?

Have the cares and busyness of life and the desire for success left God standing on the outside of our lives?

Has the one and only God of the Bible become second to another the god called Social Media?

Did you know almighty God can make something beautiful out of something as horrific as a pandemic?

What would this world look like if every eye and every heart turned towards Jesus?

📕 - 2 Chronicles 7:14 (GNT) 14–"If they pray to me and repent and turn away from the evil they have been doing, then I will hear them in heaven, forgive their sins, and make their land prosperous again."

💭 - God hears your prayers. He can heal anyone at any time on His timetable. You are reading this book because the Lord Jesus has touched your heart and His Spirit has drawn you to this book.

Things may not look so wonderful as we head into another year, and the way of life doesn't look like it did prior to 2019, but we're all adjusting to a new way of life and recovery is looking better and better.

God has an **amazing** plan for your life:

📕 – Jeremiah 29:11 (NLT)–"For I know the plans I have for you," says the LORD. "They are plans for good and not for disaster, to give you a future and a hope."

💭 - The answers to life's questions can be found between the front and back covers of this devotional.

Trust in the Lord for everything and He will make your way prosperous.

Week 1
THE CHALLENGES OF LIFE: GOD HEARS YOUR PRAYERS

About 30 years ago, my closest childhood friend was in the midst of a crisis. We were in our mid-twenties, and as we **all know**, real life begins with adult responsibilities.

My friend lived alone in a nice apartment, had a sporty car, and a job that sufficiently enabled him to meet his needs.

He is the kind of person everyone enjoys being around and has the uncanny ability to tell a story that keeps his listeners captivated and eager for the climax. He's incredibly funny and takes the time to listen to the concerns of those who are hurting or experiencing life difficulties. My friend speaks with great wisdom, has compassion towards all who are suffering, and will go out of his way to lend a helping hand. He's loyal to his employer, works with integrity, and most importantly, loves the Lord Jesus.

This particular time in his life found him on the side of difficulty and trial. Compassion and caring being his strong suit, he's not so ready to receive assistance from others. In fact, when he's experiencing difficulties, he will not mention it often choosing to go it alone.

One day, I asked him, "How's everything going on the job?"

He responded, "I'm not working right now."

I asked, "How long have you been out of work?"

He answered, "A few weeks."

I replied, "Man, why didn't you tell me sooner?"

He answered, "I'll be alright."

I asked, "What can I do, what do you need?"

He answered, "I'll let you know, don't worry."

Several weeks passed; during that time, I'd drop by his apartment to check on him to see how he was doing, and what he needed. He refused to accept assistance, but he'd occasionally ask me to bring him a burger 🍔 as I pass through on my way home from work.

Approaching two months, with no job and nothing promising on the horizon, he showed no signs of panic. I couldn't believe the peace and calm he displayed. I would've pulled my hair out.

He did have food in his pantry, that consisted of a few cans of Vienna sausages, a jar of peanut butter, oatmeal, rice, and, of course, several packs of "RAMEN." In his refrigerator, there were fixings for sandwiches, sodas, and lots of empty space.

In the midst of the second month, he told me that he had an interview, and he's excited about it, and it's suitable. I was thrilled and eager for a wonderful outcome. A week later, I paid him a visit and inquired about the result of the interview.

He said, "They offered me the job and the pay is really good."

I shouted joyfully, "THAT'S GREAT!"

He replied, "But I declined."

I responded loudly, **"What! Are you kidding? Don't you need a job? What are you doing? You've been without a job for two months!"**

His calm response to my many questions was very profound, "Derv (short for Dervon) yes, the position was mine for the taking and the salary was really good, but a job is a marriage between the employer and the employee, so while the employer was interviewing me to see if I was the right partner for the job, I was interviewing the employer. I determined it wasn't the right fit for me."

I asked, "How could you be so sure you made the right decision?"

He replied, "Days leading up to the interview, including the day of the interview, I was in prayer asking the Lord for wisdom and discernment."

I was speechless. In my mind, I thought, "Man, that's a huge mistake!"

Sometime afterward, he landed a job suitable for him, and now, thirty years later, he's still in the same industry and a much higher position. glory to God.

During the challenges of life,
God hears your prayers.

Reflect
DAY 1:
DO NOT WORRY ABOUT TOMORROW

- Matthew 6:34 (NLT)–"So don't worry about tomorrow, for tomorrow will bring its own worries. Today's trouble is enough for today."

💭 - Think of a time when you were traveling, and in the distance, a mountain or skyscraper was in clear view. The mountain or skyscraper didn't seem so grand from a distance, but as you drew near, your eyes focused, and the object grew.

The moment you were in close proximity, your eyes widen, glued on the mountain or skyscraper, and you began to take in the enormity of the structure.

Ask Yourself…

Well, do I remember my perspective of the mountain or skyscraper from a distance?

Did the mountain/building actually grow?

Do I recall my laser focus on the object?

After passing the mountain/skyscraper, did it chase me?

Did this massive object decrease in scope as I traveled forward?

Did this enormous structure eventually disappear as I continued to travel?

We all face enormous challenges in our lives and these challenges seem immovable like Mt. Kilimanjaro and the Empire State Building, however, Jesus encourages us **not to worry.**

*Did you know that 90 percent of the things we worry about **never** actually happen?*

We have the tendency to stress over things that are days ahead, however, Jesus says don't worry about tomorrow!

Why?

1) Because we can't change tomorrow; we can only respond to today.
2) Because Jesus commands us not to worry. Worry is a sin. Worry means that we allow fear to set in and we aren't trusting in Jesus; thus Jesus is **smaller** than our problem.

When you keep Jesus at the center of your day, The Holy Spirit (the Spirit of the Lord Jesus) will guide you in the proper approach to your problems. Jesus will never abandon you, and He's **more** than able to move the mountains and skyscrapers out of your path so you may travel on to the next day and the next day and the next day filled with His peace.

Before you begin your day, talk to God about your tomorrow because He hears your prayers. Then go through your day and do not worry about tomorrow.

Reflect
DAY 2:
GIVE ALL YOUR WORRIES AND CARES TO GOD

-1 Peter 5:7 (NLT)–"Give all your worries and cares to God, for he cares about you."

- This is a soothing, but power-packed scripture. The Lord commands us **to give all**. All doesn't mean a little, some, or a lot.

It means to give **all** your worries. It's okay to have concerns or cares, but your concerns can become your worries if your concerns **consume** you, filling your mind more than anything else.

- Worry: To torment oneself with or suffer from disturbing thoughts.

This scripture brings a brighter revelation because after **"worries"** it reads **"and cares."** The word "and" is the conjunction connecting what was said prior, and says "along with or in addition to." God desires you to give Him **all** your tormenting thoughts **and all** your cares. He is so compassionate towards you that He invites you to give Him **everything** that is a load on your mind and He will take care of it all. He wants His children to be worry-free, filled with peace and clarity of mind, and flowing in life with joy.

Why?

Because He cares for you.

Care has several definitions, but the appropriate definition at this point in this scripture is:

Dictionary - The provision of what is needed for the well-being and or protection of a person or thing.

Thought - It's comforting and amazing to know you/we are loved so much by the Savior of the world, that He not only took all of our sins upon Himself, but He commands us to give Him our worries, too. You can count on Him to provide you with the perfect solution to your worries whatever that may be.

He is faithful, He is true, He is love, and He cares for you.

As you begin this day, give all of your concerns about life's challenges to God because He cares for you and hears your prayers. Before you close your eyes tonight, thank Him for being there for you through all the challenges of life.

Reflect
DAY 3: GOD WILL RESCUE YOU FROM ALL YOUR TROUBLES

-Psalm 34:17 (NLT)–"The LORD hears his people when they call to him for help. He rescues them from all their troubles."

- We've all faced countless days when we cried out for help. We usually cry out for help to a friend, family member, coworker, and possibly a professional.

In my own life, I've faced many difficulties and have been placed in seemingly insurmountable situations, while placing the Lord last on my list to cry out to. The aforementioned list couldn't help me, but the Lord delivered. He has pulled me and my family out of certain financial ruin. It was truly miraculous.

How did I know it was the Lord?

When the Lord comes to the rescue, He will deliver you in such a way that you will know a human being couldn't have done it. The Holy Spirit will assure you that it was the hands of the Lord Almighty! Working on your behalf. He will blow your mind.

When the challenges in my life were crushing me, I was delivered from certain devastation **only when I cried out to the Lord FIRST!**

I must admit, though, for twenty years of my life I've experienced seasons where the Lord never entered my thoughts. I was doing my own thing, my own way, trusting in my own abilities, and faced with extreme trials.

The Lord used my son Justin to touch my heart and guide me to recommit my life to Jesus and rescue me. Once I made this recommitment, I began to realize that placing the Lord **first** in all things brings peace, calmness, and a flow of joy. The eyes of my heart were beginning to open more to the ways of the Lord, and when the difficulties of life stood before me, the Lord Jesus was/is the clear choice of rescue and deliverance.

He shows Himself mighty in our weaknesses and times of desperation.

If you have a relationship with the Lord and are faced with major challenges, I want to assure you He will deliver you because He's faithful to His word and promises. His rescue may not be what you envision, but He is with you in your present struggles and He was with you in your past difficulties.

He carried you through, doing the subtle things you probably overlooked. If you look back on your life, you will see He has rescued you countless times from disaster, even the disasters you weren't aware of.

The scripture says, "He rescues them from all their troubles."

*Thank the Lord today because He is faithful to His Word, and He will hear you and rescue you from **all** your troubles no matter what you are facing this day.*

Reflect
DAY 4:
GOD WILL NOT ABANDON YOU

- Psalm 34:19 (NLT)–"The righteous person faces many troubles, but the LORD comes to the rescue each time."

- Our Lord Jesus is compassionate and attentive. He always hears the prayers of His saints and is thrilled when we bring our concerns to Him.

In the Lord's eyes, those who have placed their faith in Him are righteous. He will not allow the godly to slip and fall.

We all will face troubles and challenges throughout life, but the Lord makes it clear in Psalm 34:19 that He comes to the rescue of the righteous each time.

Are you righteous?

All believers have the same Heavenly Father and Savior, the Lord Jesus.

Do you recall your childhood years as your parents gave you assurance on certain things—like dinner on the table, materials for school projects, and help with the project?

How about your parents giving you assurance after suffering a small injury, that everything will be just fine?

How about the fear of receiving that dreadful shot in the doctor's office, performing in a school play, etc.?

Your parents always comforted you, promised safety in tight situations, and assured you they'd always be there for you.

Your loving Heavenly Father is your greater parent. He's not human, so He cannot lie, nor will He change His mind (Numbers 23:19). He is faithful to His word and His promises.

Psalm 34:19 is just one of the thousands of God's promises.

Think back to a time when you were faced with a seemingly insurmountable challenge and certain for disaster.

Ask Yourself…

When I cried out or prayed to the Lord, what did He do?

How did that so-called "certain doom" work out?

You survived that catastrophe and several other unfortunate circumstances.

So why do you worry?

The Lord has rescued you in the past, He will rescue you in today's troubles, and He will rescue you tomorrow. His track record is impeccable.

How can you be certain of His rescue?

The second half of Psalm 34:19 says, "But the Lord comes (continuously and present tense) to the rescue each time."

Rescue is defined as to free or deliver from confinement, danger, or difficulty.

However, being in the midst of a difficult situation, your vision of being rescued may be realized differently than you expect.

God's plan for your rescue involves much more than what you see in front of you.

Sometimes, the Lord delivers you from certain doom **supernaturally**.

Sometimes, He allows you to go through the fires of trials for your development, but He's moving things out of your way (behind the scenes; dangers in the trial that are unseen); He will **not** allow you to be burned as you go through.

Sometimes, the Lord will bring someone into your circumstance (friend, family, coworker, neighbor.. etc.) with the perfect solution, words of encouragement, comfort, and or a helping/saving hand.

The Lord comes to the rescue each time!

God's plan for you usually involves other people. Others witness the wonderful work being done in your life, and they, too, are touched as they take their role in your rescue.

If your circumstance appears dire to those around you, your deliverance will bring glory to God, increase your faith in Him, and possibly draw those around you who don't believe in Him.

Remember God's promise to be with you and not abandon you (Deuteronomy 31:8). Thank Him that He comes to the rescue each time you face a challenge.

Reflect
DAY 5:
GOD KNOWS YOUR NEEDS

- Matthew 6:8 (NLT)–"Don't be like them, for your Father knows exactly what you need even before you ask him!"

💭 - isn't it comforting to know that the lines of communication to our Heavenly Father are ALWAYS open?

It's wonderful to know that our Heavenly Father, ALREADY knows what we need before we ask. We don't have to give him a long drawn out prayer filled with 10,000 empty words.

Many believe that an effective prayer is a prayer with more words; prayer time is information time—our time to inform the Lord of our problems which He is clueless about–right?

Not so. Our Heavenly Father is OMNISCIENT- all knowing. He's not impressed with lots of meaningless repetitive words–don't babble, and don't give Him a lecture. When we pray; Simply enter His presence, address Him properly, confess our sins and trespasses, share our concerns with Him, make our requests, acknowledge the person(Jesus) who gives us access to the Father, and express our confidence in our prayer with an AMEN (it is so).

So why pray if He already knows?

Firstly, the Lord responds to prayer. Prayer is your heart connecting with His heart. Our Heavenly Father desires relationship; and there's no relationship without communication. Secondly, if we don't ask, we MAY not receive:

- Matthew 7:8 (NLT) For everyone who asks, receives. Everyone who seeks, finds. And to everyone who knocks, the door will be opened.

- Let's take a look from this perspective:

Parents have a God-given gift of intuition especially as it pertains to their children's activities and needs.

Parents have this keen sense of awareness (a gift of God) of their child's whereabouts and unauthorized dealings. Parents are aware of their child's needs even before their child/children make mention of the need.

Followers of Jesus Christ have an eternal parent. Your Heavenly Father is the almighty and all-knowing God.

He knows what you need before you ask Him. He has promised to provide all of your **needs**, but not your **greeds**.

📖 - Philippians 4:19 (NLT)–"And this same God who takes care of me will supply all your needs from his glorious riches, which have been given to us in Christ Jesus."

Parents, I'm certain you make sure that at least one meal is provided daily for your children. It may not be gourmet, but it's a meal.

Are your children worried about having a daily meal?

I'm positive you make sure your children are clothed. It may not be the latest high-end designer apparel, but they're clothed.

Are your children distraught over going a day without any clothing?

📖 - Matthew 6:28-30 (NLT)- 28–"And why worry about your clothing? Look at the lilies of the field and how they grow. They don't work or make their clothing,

📖 - 29 yet Solomon in all his glory was not dressed as beautifully as they are.

📖 - 30 And if God cares so wonderfully for wildflowers that are here today and thrown into the fire tomorrow, he will certainly care for you. Why do you have so little faith?"

💭 - The child/children of loving parents aren't concerned with their needs being met. They will live life in confidence because they **know** their parents are in control.

It's the same in your relationship with your Heavenly Father. He **knows** all and sees all. He is your provider and protector. All you need to do is seek Him **first**, and He will take care of the rest.

- Matthew 6:33 (NLT)–"Seek the Kingdom of God above all else, and live righteously, and he will give you everything you need."

- For those who are **not** a child of God, these things are **not promised**. To be a child of God, you must accept Jesus, His Son, as your Lord and Savior. God loves all of His creation, and He's waiting with open arms to lavish **all** with blessings.

The life of the nonbeliever is a life of self-reliance, mixed with uncertainty, and the yo-yo effect (ups and downs). When life takes a turn in the wrong direction or finances have gone awry, a nonbeliever has no one to trust when self-reliance fails. Worry sets in, bad choices become the only choice, which leads to compromise, misery, and chaos.

No matter what you are facing today, trust in Jesus, give Him your worries and receive all that He has for you for He hears your prayers and truly cares for you.

Reflect
DAY 6:
THE LORD DELIGHTS IN ANSWERING PRAYERS

-Proverbs 15:29 (CEV)–"The LORD never even hears the prayers of the wicked, but he answers the prayers of all who obey him."

- *So, who does the Lord consider wicked?*

Jesus sacrificed His perfect and **sinless life** on the cross by taking upon Himself, all the sins we have committed in the past, the sins we will commit today, and in the future.

Jesus did this out of His love for every human being; so that mankind will have a relationship with Him for eternity and NOT suffer eternal punishment.

Jesus made the **"great exchange."**

He took all of your sins and gave you His righteousness. It's His **free gift**. No one deserves this gift, and no one can earn it.

Now, when Almighty God looks at you, He sees Jesus.

However, it's up to each person to accept this free gift of salvation. Those who reject this gift; almighty God **considers that person wicked.**

All who accept Jesus as Lord and savior of their lives is forgiven of every sin. Those are who God **considers righteous. The righteous, over time, learn obedience as their relationship with the Lord grows.**

We know Almighty God sees everything and hears everything, but this scripture is saying He is not **obligated** to answer the prayers of the sinner(the wicked, the non-believer). The Lord God is loving, gracious, and merciful. When a sinner (a person who hasn't accepted His Son Jesus as Lord and Savior into their heart) prays for salvation and repents of his/her sins, God answers with a resounding **"yes."**

The Lord **always** answers the prayers of those who are obedient to Him (believers-His children). When faced with difficulties, regardless of the severity, the Lord will certainly answer. While in the midst of your prayer He may ask you, "Is there anything too hard for the Lord?"

- Genesis 8:13-14 (NLT) 13 –"Then the LORD said to Abraham, 'Why did Sarah laugh? Why did she say, 'Can an old woman like me have a baby?'

📖 - 14 Is anything too hard for the LORD? I will return about this time next year, and Sarah will have a son."

💭 - Those who have placed their faith in the Lord Jesus can approach Him at any time in prayer with complete confidence as they ask for the desires of their heart.

If you don't ask, you may not receive. Remember, your motives must be pure.

📖 - James 4:2-3 (NLT) 2 –"You want what you don't have, so you scheme and kill to get it. You are jealous of what others have, but you can't get it, so you fight and wage war to take it away from them. Yet you don't have what you want because you don't ask God for it.

📖 - 3 And even when you ask, you don't get it because your motives are all wrong—you want only what will give you pleasure."

💭 - I want to encourage persistence in your prayers. It's okay to pray for the same thing over and over. As a matter of fact, the Lord tells us to **keep asking**:

📖 - Matthew 7:7 (NLT)–"Keep on asking, and you will receive what you ask for. Keep on seeking, and you will find. Keep on knocking, and the door will be opened to you."

Follow the Lord's instructions in Matthew 7:7 all throughout your day knowing He delights in answering your prayers. Thank Him before you close your eyes tonight for answering your prayers.

DAY 7: MY JOURNAL

This week, you learned you can give all of your concerns about life's challenges to God because He cares for you, hears your prayers, will rescue you, and will never abandon you.

Remember, when worry sets in, bad choices lead to compromise, misery, and chaos. Therefore, do not worry.

Record in your journal the insights and answers to prayer you received throughout this week. Thank Him for always being there with you through all of life's challenges.

_____

_____

_____

_____

_____

_____

_____

_____

_____

_____

Week 2
WHAT IS THE DIFFERENCE BETWEEN KNOWLEDGE OF GOD'S WORD AND UNDERSTANDING GOD'S WORD?

- Reading God's Word and listening to a pastor is vital in the life of the believer. Knowledge and understanding are key.

However, there's a stark difference between knowledge and understanding.

Knowledge is stored information that doesn't do anything; sort of like the canned goods in your kitchen cabinet that have been there for years.

- Knowledge:

1) the body of truths or facts accumulated in the course of time.
2) acquaintance or familiarity gained by sight, experience, or report.
3) the sum of what is known.

💭 - In 2010, I recommitted my life to Christ. In doing so, the Holy Spirit led me to purchase a Bible (for the first time) and begin reading. In the beginning, my reading and understanding of the Bible was quite a challenge. Reading the Bible is unlike any other book, but in the beginning, nothing made sense to me.

The Bible seemed like a bunch of words thrown together.

In one of his sermons, the pastor said, "When reading your Bible, and you come across a verse that seems confusing, don't give up. Keep reading." Timely, right?

A week later, on my drive home from work, I was listening to a Christian radio station that broadcasts different pastors giving sermons every half hour all day. The pastor spoke about reading the Bible and said, "When you read something that doesn't make sense to you, read it over and over. Meditate on it, but don't get stuck. After you've read it a few times, move on, but come back to it another day." Timely, right?

I followed the advice of each pastor regarding reading the Bible. It was still frustrating, but the Holy Spirit encouraged me and strengthened me to continue.

Another day, on my commute to work, wouldn't you know a different pastor spoke on reading the Bible. This pastor emphatically said, "**Make it a point to commit to memory,** one scripture at each reading. Over time, these scriptures will come to mind when you need to share them with someone. Over time, you will gain understanding." Timely, right?

I immediately began to follow this pastor's words of wisdom. I began writing down the scriptures that **grabbed my attention** during my daily reading on the blank pages of my Bible. I read these scriptures over and over, committed them to memory, but it was all knowledge. I wanted and needed **understanding.**

 - Understanding:

1) superior power of discernment; enlightened intelligence:
2) mental process of a person who comprehends; comprehension; personal interpretation:
3) comprehend is to understand the nature or meaning of; grasp with the mind; take in or embrace it.

- Biblical understanding begins with your brain. The brain is a mighty organ that transmits and delivers messages to every part of our bodies creating movements. The brain stores information, processes it, and transforms it into knowledge.

Behind your physical brain is your **mind**, your spiritual brain, your conscience. Your **mind** reasons the right things to do (righteous living), and the wrong things to do (sinful).

Behind your physical heart is your spiritual heart.

Your spiritual heart receives information from your spiritual brain and converts this information into understanding.

Knowledge is information stored in your physical brain.

Understanding is from your spiritual heart which is how you reason any matter and how you operate your life.

The Bible is **unlike** any other book. The words come alive, are powerful, and they touch and move the heart, tingling the soul. Sort of like an "Awww-yes" moment, but much more often.

God's word, the Bible, is so rich with so much depth that a person can **only** navigate through life successfully by reading it.

📖 - 2 Timothy 3:16 (NLT) – "All Scripture is inspired by God and is useful to teach us what is true and to make us realize what is wrong in our lives. It corrects us when we are wrong and teaches us to do what is right."

📖 - Joshua 1:8 (NLT) – "Study this Book of Instruction continually. Meditate on it day and night so you will be sure to obey everything written in it. Only then will you prosper and succeed in all you do."

💭 - No one can ever gain a complete understanding of the entire Bible because it is inexhaustible. Each scripture has so much depth, so much enjoyment, and so much life.

As for me, the Bible has brought clarity to my life. I no longer see and navigate life as I did before my relationship with Christ. The light bulb comes on at every reading. It illuminates my heart and allows me to understand how much Jesus loves me and every human being. Only the Lord and His word can take me to a higher level of understanding His heart for the world and His **purpose**

for my life. I now live a life of joy and peace; although that doesn't mean I don't have problems and issues. I now navigate life in peace and understanding. In my knowledge and understanding of God's Word, I'm further along than I was in the beginning, twelve years ago, and I still have a long way to go.

While you're gaining knowledge, seek understanding.

- James 1:22-23 (NLT)

22 – "But don't just listen to God's word. You must do what it says. Otherwise, you are only fooling yourselves.

- 23 For if you listen to the word and don't obey, it is like glancing at your face in a mirror."

- Understanding God's Word permeates every fiber of your HEART  and your being.

- Ezekiel 3:10 (NLT)–Then he added, "Son of man, let all my words sink deep into your own heart first. Listen to them carefully for yourself."

- Understanding originates from **your strong desire to know Jesus in every way possible.**

Pressure to Purpose

💭 - This desire will lead to seeking the Lord in prayer, meditating on the word of God daily, and living out His instructions for our lives.

📖 - Proverbs 8:17 (NLT)-17 "I love all who love me. Those who search will surely find me."

💭 - Proverbs 8:17 is **wisdom** speaking to YOU. True wisdom comes from God; wisdom is in His being. When you seek wisdom, understanding is received. Understanding gives the believer's heart ❤, eyes to see life from a godly perspective, and ears to hear the voice of the Holy Spirit in a more intimate way as He guides our lives.

📖 - Matthew 13:13-16 (NLT) 13 –"That is why I use these parables, For they look, but they don't really see. They hear, but they don't really listen or understand.

📖 - 14 This fulfills the prophecy of Isaiah that says, 'When you hear what I say, you will not understand. When you see what I do, you will not comprehend.

📖 - 15 For the hearts of these people are hardened, and their ears cannot hear, and they have closed their eyes— so their eyes cannot see, and their ears cannot hear, and their hearts cannot understand, and they cannot turn to me and let me heal them.'

📕 - 16 But blessed are your eyes, because they see; and your ears, because they hear."

💭 - Once understanding sets in, the believer desires to live the life that our Heavenly Father has preplanned for him/her (becoming a doer).

📕 - Ephesians 2:10 (GNT)–"God has made us what we are, and in our union with Christ Jesus he has created us for a life of good deeds, which he has already prepared for us to do."

💭 - Understanding from the heart ❤️ leads to seeking a deeper relationship with your Lord and Savior, thus allowing Him to be the Lord of your life, and following His commandments to become a bright shining star for His glorious kingdom.

📕 - John 14:21 (NLT) – "Those who accept my commandments and obey them are the ones who love me. And because they love me, my Father will love them. And I will love them and reveal myself to each of them."

So, let's discover what the difference between the knowledge of God's Word and understanding God's Word means in our everyday lives.

Meditate
DAY 1: UNDERSTANDING GOD'S WORD

- Ezekiel 3:10 (NLT)–Then he added, "Son of man, let all my words sink deep into your own heart first. Listen to them carefully for yourself."

💭 - Understanding requires meditation; to focus on what is in front of you or what you're reading or listening to and allowing it to simmer into your heart.

Think of the Word of God as a meal, and the roast is the main course.

To get the desired results, would you cook the roast in a microwave?

More than likely you'd place your roast in a crockpot with shallow water, surrounded with veggies, and sprinkled or rubbed with your desired seasonings. You'd then allow the roast to simmer for hours until every ingredient makes its way into every ounce of the roast. When it's time to feast on the main course, the roast is extremely tender, flavored perfectly, melts in your mouth, completely satisfies you as you slowly chew.

It's the same way with the Word of God. You are to allow God's Word to permeate **every** fiber of your being, bringing you into an understanding of His heart for you and your life.

It's so important to read, study, and meditate on His Word as often as possible, preferably in the morning before you begin your day. Ask God to bring you into understanding more and more about His heart for you and your life.

Meditate
DAY 2:
DESIRE, LISTEN, UNDERSTAND

-Matthew 13:12 (NLT) – "To those who listen to my teaching, more understanding will be given, and they will have an abundance of knowledge. But for those who are not listening, even what little understanding they have will be taken away from them."

💭 - Since understanding originates from your strong desire to know Jesus in every way possible, you will desire to closely **listen** to His words thus receiving an understanding of the heart of God.

Hearing is **not** the **same** as **listening** to the Word of God. When a person's heart is closed (hardened) to Jesus, whatever he or she hears through the physical ear will **not** reach the heart. Those whose hearts are pliable will allow the ears of their heart to listen and the eyes of their heart to see; an enlightened heart is a understanding heart.

The more someone desires to know Jesus, the more he or she will listen to His word (teaching), and the more understanding will be given.

Anyone who chooses **not** to listen and has chosen to turn their hearts away from the Lord will **not** receive understanding and will lose what little understanding they do have.

Think of it this way. If you place your right arm in a hard cast and sling for two years, then remove the cast and sling, your right arm will be significantly smaller than your left arm. Due to your right arm being inactive, the strength in that arm will be minimal at best making it nearly useless.

The Lord longs for a relationship with each and every one of us. He has wonderful plans and blessings for us, but we will never realize His loving plan for our lives if we choose **not** to listen to Him. He wants to pour His love into our hearts so that we can share His love with others. The Lord wants to partner with us in a loving and powerful way.

*As you begin your day, open your heart to the Lord, so your spiritual ears can hear and **listen** to the voice of the Holy Spirit. Ask Him to open your spiritual eyes so you can see and understand what He desires to reveal to you.*

Desire, Listen, and Understand!

Meditate
DAY 3:
SEEK WISDOM

-Proverbs 2:6 (NLT) – "For the LORD grants wisdom! From his mouth come knowledge and understanding."

Everything we have comes from the Lord.

- Psalm 16:2 (NLT) – "I said to the LORD, 'You are my Master! Every good thing I have comes from you'."

- God/Jesus is the supplier of all wisdom and the source of knowledge and understanding.

What's wisdom?

- the ability to discern
- good sense
- good judgment
- insight

- ability to solve a problem with **little** or **no** knowledge of the matter.

How is His wisdom granted?

📖 - Psalm 111:10 (CEV) – "Respect and obey the LORD! This is the first step to wisdom and good sense. God will always be respected."

📖 - James 1:5 (NLT) If you need wisdom, ask our generous God, and he will give it to you. He will not rebuke you for asking.

📖 - 1 Corinthians 1:30 (GNT) – "But God has brought you into union with Christ Jesus, and God has made Christ to be our wisdom. By him we are put right with God; we become God's holy people and are set free."

💭 - Those who are wise will consistently seek the Lord's advice, guidance, and knowledge for everyday living.

As you **seek** the heart of the Lord for daily living, your relationship with Him grows. In this growing relationship, the Lord desires that you not only gain knowledge, but receive deep understanding. As the Holy Spirit illuminates your understanding, your knowledge **increases** in all the ways of life.

📖 - Proverbs 14:6 (NLT) – "A mocker seeks wisdom and never finds it, but knowledge comes easily to those with understanding."

Wisdom is God's perspective. Knowledge is truth rooted in knowing God and His word. Understanding is the practical application of God's wisdom and knowledge.

Seek wisdom, receive understanding, and gain knowledge.

As you begin this day, follow the pattern God has given you to gain wisdom, receive understanding, and gain knowledge to accomplish His will for you today.

Meditate
DAY 4:
SET KNOWLEDGE IN MOTION

-2 Chronicles 1:10 (NLT) – "Give me the wisdom and knowledge to lead them properly, for who could possibly govern this great people of yours?"

💭 - Knowledge is usually accompanied by other gifts such as wisdom, understanding, discernment, or good judgment.

God's gift of knowledge is rarely given by itself. Knowledge by itself is useless until it's tied with another gift and set in motion.

Think of a computer. It's basically a storage unit for an enormous amount of information, but it is useless until someone turns on the power and accesses the information needed to perform certain functions.

The one and only God of the Bible is a giver. He gives to all of His creation, and certainly to those who believe in His Son, Jesus.

The knowledge given to the believer is to bring glory to God, but this gift of knowledge is extremely beneficial for the children of God as well.

Knowledge used in the right way (godly way), and not for evil or selfish ambitions, will open the doors of opportunity and touch the lives of others surrounding you.

The Lord has placed you where you are in your life right now—vocation, education, leadership, congress, local government official, and the city of residence to use the gift of knowledge and other gifts He has given you to make a difference.

In 2 Chronicles 1:10, King Solomon is in prayer asking for wisdom and knowledge to lead the nation of Israel God's way. It's important to notice that King Solomon sought the Lord **first**, and for the right reason. This pleased the Lord.

📖 - 2 Chronicles 1:11-12 (NLT) 11 – "God said to Solomon, 'Because your greatest desire is to help your people, and you did not ask for wealth, riches, fame, or even the death of your enemies or a long life, but rather you asked for wisdom and knowledge to properly govern my people'."

📖 - 12 – "I will certainly give you the wisdom and knowledge you requested. But I will also give you wealth, riches, and fame such as no other king has had before you or will ever have in the future!"

💭 - The key is to seek a relationship with Jesus and the heart of the Father **above anything else**.

Your life will be enriched beyond measure, then understanding and knowledge will overflow. Your life will be filled with the excellent knowledge of living a godly marriage, being a godly parent, being a godly employee, a godly employer, a godly business owner, a godly local and national leader, and so much more!

Seek the Lord.
Listen closely.
Receive understanding.
Knowledge will overflow.
Set knowledge in motion.
Change the world.

This is God's plan for you today, so listen closely as He shows you how to set the knowledge He has given you in motion and begin to change the area of the world He has given you influence over.

Meditate

DAY 5: UNDERSTAND THE FULLNESS AND PURPOSE FOR LIFE

- Daniel 5:12 (NLT) – "This man Daniel, whom the king named Belteshazzar, has exceptional ability and is filled with divine knowledge and understanding. He can interpret dreams, explain riddles, and solve difficult problems. Call for Daniel, and he will tell you what the writing means."

💭 - Science tells us that humans use **only** 10 percent of the brain.

What about the other 90 percent?

I recall a fascinating movie back in 2011 titled "LIMITLESS" starring Bradley Cooper. In this entertaining, but thought-provoking film, Bradley Cooper is given a pill that would give him the ability to use a greater percentage of his brain. Within minutes of consuming the pill, his thinking became clearer than ever, he completes writing the manuscript to his novel in just a couple of days, calculates extremely difficult mathematical problems at warp speed, speaks several foreign languages fluently, plays musical instruments he'd never before considered with precision, becomes an expert stock market consultant, has the ability to see things and situations before it happens. His knowledge and understanding became **Limitless**.

Yes, I know that's Hollywood and movie magic, but the Word of God and the power of God are **true**.

The power of God, the Holy Spirit, dwells within every person who asks Jesus for the forgiveness of sins and accepts Him as Savior and Lord of their lives.

The Holy Spirit operates within the believer teaching every believer everything he or she needs to know about the heart of Jesus and guides them to live righteously.

- 1 John 2:27 (NLT) – "But you have received the Holy Spirit, and he lives within you, so you don't need anyone to teach you what is true. For the Spirit teaches you everything you need to know, and what he teaches is true—it is not a lie. So just as he has taught you, remain in fellowship with Christ."

- The Holy Spirit is the third person of the Godhead. The trinity is three distinct persons (God the Father, God the Son, God the Holy Spirit) operating in different functions while working in unison. The three are the **same**—three in one and one in three.

📖 - Romans 8:9 (NLT) – "But you are not controlled by your sinful nature. You are controlled by the Spirit if you have the Spirit of God living in you. (And remember that those who do not have the Spirit of Christ living in them do not belong to him at all.)"

💭 - Jesus, the Son of God, and God the Father are one.

📖 - John 10:30 (NLT)–"The Father and I are one."

💭 - Wisdom and insight come from the Lord.

📖 - Job 32:8 (MSG) – "But I see I was wrong—it's God's Spirit in a person, the breath of the Almighty One, that makes wise human insight possible."

💭 - Those who are in a relationship with the Lord Jesus don't need a pill. The believer only needs the Lord. The Lord will unlock the limits of the brain, mind, and heart to levels beyond the imagination.

Seeking the heart of God and desiring to grow in a relationship with Him allows Him to pour into you, divine knowledge and understanding.

In Daniel 5:12, Daniel was a Hebrew taken into captivity along with the citizens of Jerusalem by the Babylonians to become their slaves.

Daniel's faithfulness and obedience to the Lord made it possible for Daniel's gifts (divine knowledge and understanding) to grab the attention of the king of Babylon.

- Proverbs 18:16 (NKJV) – "A man's gift makes room for him, and brings him before great men."

- Over time, Daniel was elevated over many highly respected officials and trusted men of the king, to interpret dreams and advise on difficult matters. Today, Daniel would be considered a consultant in the president's cabinet.

As you seek the knowledge of Christ today, receive the fullness, understanding, and purpose of life God has put in place for you. Thank Him for His guidance and the divine knowledge and understanding He has given you.

Meditate
DAY 6: BECOMING A SERVANT OF THE LORD

- Jeremiah 3:15 (NLT) – "And I will give you shepherds after my own heart, who will guide you with knowledge and understanding."

💭 - In this scripture, the Lord is speaking to the backslidden nation of Israel, but also applicable for everyone today.

The Lord provides pastors, church leaders, and teachers of the Word of God as shepherds after His own heart. They will guide and care for the concerns and needs of the people spiritually and physically, with the knowledge and understanding of the heart of God.

The Holy Spirit empowers the shepherd to do the work of the Lord by feeding the flock (believers, the church) the gospel and the goodness of God by the Word of God. These shepherds are to help the flock cultivate a relationship with the Lord, equip the flock to do the work of the Lord, and carefully guide the flock through the difficulties of life.

Our earthly shepherds are to be carbon copies of our **Great Shepherd**, the Lord Jesus.

📖 - Psalm 23:1-4 (GNT) 1 – "The LORD is my shepherd; I have everything I need.

📖 - 2 He lets me rest in fields of green grass and leads me to quiet pools of fresh water.

📖 - 3 He gives me new strength. He guides me in the right paths, as he has promised.

📖 - 4 Even if I go through the deepest darkness, I will not be afraid, LORD, for you are with me. Your shepherd's rod and staff protect me."

💭 - As we meditate and chew on the Word of God, we must understand that consuming it and storing it is only **knowledge** gained. We must put it into practice. A necessary component to understanding is application—**doing**.

📖 - Luke 11:28 (NLT) – "Jesus replied, 'But even more blessed are all who hear the word of God and put it into practice'."

💭 - As you continually listen to, meditate on, and apply the Word of God to your life, you will live a more fulfilling and purposeful life.

Being a part of God's family, learning together, and gathering in fellowship is vital in the life of the believer. Just as we are a part of and work together in our personal family life, we are to operate with our brothers and sisters in the family of Christ.

There's so much that will take place over the course of our lives we will not understand; thus, the necessity of a Spirit-led leader. We are to look to a shepherd who lives his life the way the Lord expects him to live it and teaches the way the Holy Spirit leads him to teach to help us receive clarity and understanding in our life's journey.

📖 - Titus1:6-8 (GNT) 6 – "an elder must be without fault; he must have only one wife, and his children must be believers and not have the reputation of being wild or disobedient.

📖 - 7–For since a church leader is in charge of God's work, he should be without fault. He must not be arrogant or quick-tempered, or a drunkard or violent or greedy for money.

📖 - 8–He must be hospitable and love what is good. He must be self-controlled, upright, holy, and disciplined."

📕 - Titus 1:9 (MSG) – "and have a good grip on the Message, knowing how to use the truth to either spur people on in knowledge or stop them in their tracks if they oppose it."

💭 - As the shepherd of the Lord's flock leads with the knowledge of the heart of Christ and with understanding, we are to listen, read, meditate, chew on, consume, and then become a doer of His Word. Every adult is a shepherd in some way- a parent, teacher, manager, supervisor, entrepreneur, coach, etc.

Do you shepherd with the heart of Christ?

Do you lead and feed, as you are being led and fed?

As you strive to be a mighty servant of the Lord, He will guide you to change the world one person at a time, one day at a time.

DAY 7:
MY JOURNAL

This week, you learned the importance of distinguishing the difference between the knowledge of God's Word and truly understanding His Word.

As you sought the knowledge of Christ, record what He revealed about His purpose of life He has put in place for you. Thank Him for His guidance and the divine knowledge and understanding He has given you.

_____

_____

_____

_____

_____

_____

_____

_____

_____

_____

Week 3
INTIMACY AND THE MOUNTAIN

📖 - Intimacy:

1) a close, familiar, and usually affectionate or loving personal relationship with another person or group.
2) a close association with or detailed knowledge or deep understanding of a place, subject, period of history, etc.
3) the quality of being comfortable, warm, or familiar.
4) privacy, especially as suitable to the telling of a secret.

💭 - My wife, Tavia, and I met thirty-seven years ago in 1985 at a party. Our relationship sparked right from the start, and we committed to dating each other solely.

We totally enjoyed getting to know one another as friends get to know one another. Tavia and I would spend countless hours in conversation over the telephone when we could not spend time with each other face to face. The next best thing was to hear each other's voice by telephone ☎.

As we became more acquainted with each other, the more time we desired to spend together. We lived in different cities, so during the week our time was spent doing life, but when the weekend rolled around, we couldn't wait to see each other. We'd eagerly plan our weekend in advance, but once we were together, time seemed to travel faster than the speed of light.

As our relationship grew, our feelings moved to another, deeper level. We would talk about any and everything, we held hands and embraced often. The weekdays were difficult for me. I wasn't the same when I was apart from her. I longed for her. We'd share things about ourselves no one else knew. The more time we shared, the more we revealed the secret places of our hearts with each other. Those moments were so special, so intimate.

Tavia and I were married in October of 1988 and now have four amazing adult children and two grandchildren.

Would you believe we still talk about any and everything?

Would you believe we're still learning about each other even though we know each other?

Well, Jesus desires to have the same close relationship with each and every one of us.

He wants to be intimate with us. Jesus wants you and I to get to know Him on a deeper level, consistently growing.

Jesus desires to reveal the secret places of His heart ❤️ with us, but it's totally up to you and me to accept His invitation.

Being a follower of Jesus is **not** a religion nor rules without love. Being a believer in Jesus is to have an everlasting relationship with Him that never gets old, never grows cold, and is always getting better. Jesus wants those special moments with **you**.

Ponder
DAY 1:
MOUNTAIN TOP MOMENTS

- Matthew 17:1-3 (NLT) 1–"Six days later Jesus took Peter and the two brothers, James and John, and led them up a high mountain to be alone.

- 2 As the men watched, Jesus' appearance was transformed so that his face shone like the sun, and his clothes became as white as light.

-3 Suddenly, Moses and Elijah appeared and began talking with Jesus."

- Do you recall a time in your life when you were excited about something wonderful, and that something was very special to you, but it was too amazing to keep to yourself?

Was there an inner circle among your circle of family, friends, and acquaintances?

My guess is you shared that special something with this inner circle.

Why not with all of your friends and acquaintances?

Though you were fond of all your friends and acquaintances, but your inner circle was **special** to you. Your relationship with your inner circle was on another level, a more intimate level. This special inner circle included those who were worthy to be a part of the secret and special things in your life—intimate moments.

Jesus loved **all** twelve disciples including Judas (the betrayer). Jesus could have taken all twelve disciples with Him up the mountain, but it was Peter, James, and John who Jesus chose to take to higher heights, a higher level in their relationship, and reveal Himself in His glory. This was a once-in-a-lifetime mountain top experience for Peter, James, and John. It was a glimpse of heaven and those in heaven—an intimate moment.

- There are things Jesus wants to show you and places He wants to take you. Jesus desires a special relationship with you. He wants to share His heart with you and lead you to higher heights.

Open your heart to the Lord today, tell Him you seek to know Him intimately, and then obey His instructions. Record what you experience during your mountain top moments today and every day as you grow closer to Him.

Ponder
DAY 2:
CONTINUE CLIMBING

-Exodus 33:18, 20, 22-23 (NLT)-18 "Moses responded, 'Then show me your glorious presence.'

- 20 'But you may not look directly at my face, for no one may see me and live.

- 22 As my glorious presence passes by, I will hide you in the crevice of the rock and cover you with my hand until I have passed by.

- 23 Then I will remove my hand and let you see me from behind. But my face will not be seen'."

💭 - One of the many blessings in being in a fulfilling relationship is the joy of knowing you can reveal and share anything with one another. The secret things of the heart ❤ are open to each other. The more you get to know one another, the greater the desire becomes to share more, know more, and grow more.

In Exodus 33, Almighty God and Moses are engaged in this interesting dialogue. Moses asks the Lord certain questions that no one else in the Israelite camp would dare to ask.

Many of us have a preconceived notion that our God, the God of the Bible, is **always** looking down on mankind with a frown, ready to strike lightning at the slightest fault, but the evidence here in Exodus 33 is to the contrary. In fact, if we look closely at God's words, we may imagine His expression to be one of endearment, softness, and love.

Allow me to **assure** you, you can choose to have an amazing, personal, and intimate relationship with the Lord, too. Moses was one of the greatest men to ever live, but guess what?— Moses was human just like you and me.

The Lord desires to lavish everyone with His love, but it will never be realized if you reject His Son, Jesus. You will never experience this intimacy and joy-filled life if you choose **not** to enter into this incredible relationship. However, if you're in this relationship, then you also know that it is endless and continually climbing.

The more you know, the more you grow, and the more He will show you. Today, make a determined choice to continually seek to know Him more and more.

Ponder
DAY 3:
HEART TO HEART

John 17:20-21 (NLT)-20 "I am praying not only for these disciples but also for all who will ever believe in me through their message.

-21 I pray that they will all be one, just as you and I are one—as you are in me, Father, and I am in you. And may they be in us so that the world will believe you sent me."

- You've heard the old adage, "Relationships are built on trust." This is so true, but I believe that relationships are built on communication **first**.

Ask Yourself…

Is it really possible to begin a relationship without communication?

Is it possible to build trust without communication?

Regardless of the type of relationship you are in—dating, friendships, or business, communication is vital. As relationships grow, the level of communication deepens, trust is earned, and hearts are softened. Prayer is equally important in our relationship with Christ.

When we read the Word of God, He's **speaking** to us and His written word comes alive. We hear and absorb what He's saying. When we pray, the Lord hears. Prayer is our heart talking to His heart.

The Lord is not interested in being a mere acquaintance. He desires an intimate relationship, **not** just the casual, "hello and goodbye." He wants to share things with you that are ONLY meant for you. He wants you to share the deepest thoughts and feelings of your heart with Him as well. He wants to do so much for you, but how can He if the lines of communication are severed?

In John 17, Jesus is talking to the Father. It's quite clear that Jesus, the Son, and God the Father have an amazing relationship. The two know each other through and through because the two are one. Marriage between a man and woman is to be the same oneness as God the Father and Jesus the Son.

- Genesis 2:24 (NLT) – "This explains why a man leaves his father and mother and is joined to his wife, and the two are united into one."

- In John 17:20-21, Jesus is sharing with the Father, His love for His disciples and anyone who will ever believe in Him. Jesus desires His disciples and all believers to be **one** with each other and **one** with Him and the Father.

Ask Yourself…

Are you and Jesus mere acquaintances?

How would you describe your relationship with the Lord?

The arms of the Lord are open, and His heart is waiting for you and your heart. He wants you to know Him intimately. He wants you to be completely comfortable to share everything with Him and to ask for anything.

🖋 - John 14:14 (NLT) – "Yes, ask me for anything in my name, and I will do it!"

Before you begin this day, spend time talking to the Lord. Open your heart up to Him. He is waiting for this special time with you.

Prayer is your heart talking to His heart.

His desires will become your desires.

Ponder
DAY 4:
LEARN TO KNOW HIM

-1 Chronicles 28:9 (NLT)–"And Solomon, my son, learn to know the God of your ancestors intimately. Worship and serve him with your whole heart and a willing mind. For the Lord sees every heart and knows every plan and thought. If you seek him, you will find him. But if you forsake him, he will reject you forever."

💭 - Here, King David is having a heart-to-heart teaching moment with his son Solomon, who will succeed him as the next king. King David is emphasizing the importance of having an intimate relationship with the God of his ancestors, the Creator of the universe.

In dating, I'm certain we all agree it is a **must** to **"learn to know"** the other person.

 - Learn:

1) to gain knowledge or skill by studying, practicing, being taught, or experiencing something.
2) to cause (something) to be in your memory by studying it: Memorize
3) to hear or be told (something): to find out (something)

💭 - Desire is the catalyst to learning. Learning requires action and learning takes time.

Being in a serious relationship requires a desire to commit to the relationship from the heart.

Do you remember that certain someone?

Do you remember how the two of you connected?

Do you remember when the two of you agreed to date?

Do you remember how the two of you were committed solely to each other?

The two of you did not need to write your commitment to each other on paper in a contract.

Your heart ❤️ was in tune with the other's heart.

You began to observe and learn the person's likes and dislikes and stored that information in your memory bank.

Pressure to Purpose

You took note of the person's habits and behavior in all circumstances and stored that in your memory bank as well.

I'm beyond **certain** you closely listened to the things they shared with others and especially shared with you. You probably asked this person questions about the things you deeply desired to know. I'm 100 percent sure you committed these things to memory.

The learning process requires patience and time.

The learning process coupled with experiences and application converts to knowledge.

In today's society, to know, or knowing, and or knowledge have become a "kick the can" concept with no depth.

We often hear phrases such as, "I know that person or you know me," but an **intimate knowing** is the deepest level of knowledge of a person. It is sort of like you know, **that you know,** *that you know.*

As the learning and the knowing increase, so does your eagerness to share with one another your feelings about the special person in your life.

Learning to know, then wanting to grow, leads to desiring to show.

You desire to show that special person how much you love and care by your **willingness** to do almost anything to please them. You're all in, heart and mind.

*How do you **know** what pleases the special person in your life?*

You **learned to know,** and you no longer have to search for the things you've learned. Pleasing them becomes as natural as breathing.

If there's anything more to learn about the special person in your life, you're certainly going to seek and search out what's missing and learn everything there is to know.

Why is it so important in dating to know everything possible about the other person?

This person may be everything you've dreamed of and ever wanted. You may want to spend the rest of your life with this person.

Did you know that the Lord Jesus wants **everyone** to **learn to know** Him the same way and more?

Jesus is our **everything**. He is all we will ever need—even more than our spouse, children, parents, etc.

Jesus wants an intimate relationship with **you,** but He will not impose His will on anyone. He will wait for you until your last breath, but when you take your last breath and have **rejected** His invitation to this relationship during your life on earth, He will **not** offer it afterward.

As you begin your day, seriously consider how committed you are in your relationship with Jesus. If you have not accepted His invitation to be in a relationship with Him, make that choice today.

Ponder
DAY 5:
MOUNTAIN MOVING FAITH

-Zechariah 4:7 (NLT) – "Nothing, not even a mighty mountain, will stand in Zerubbabel's way; it will become a level plain before him! And when Zerubbabel sets the final stone of the Temple in place, the people will shout: 'May God bless it! May God bless it!'"

💭 - Zerubbabel, a Jewish governor, had the enormous **mountain** size task of rebuilding the temple of God after being demolished years prior, by the Babylonian army.

Almighty and All-loving God sends these words (Zechariah 4:7) of encouragement to Zerubbabel through the prophet, Zechariah. We also face **mountain size**  obstacles in our lives, in our marriages, our relationships, our businesses, our finances, and our health. Staying closely connected to the Lord, spending time with Him in prayer, reading His Word, listening to His soft voice, applying His instructions to our lives, and trusting Him is the antidote for any obstacle.

You may say, "Lord, this situation is too much for me. It's impossible, nothing can be done. It's hopeless!"

But the written word of God says in –Luke 1:37 (NLT) "For nothing is impossible with God."

- Philippians 4:13 (NKJV) says, "I can do all things through Christ who strengthens me."

- The Lord will flatten any mountain standing in front of you or give you the strength to climb over it.

You can trust the Lord Jesus for all things; He is faithful to His word. He will not disappoint you.

Being in constant fellowship with the Lord, seeking His heart in all matters, and moving into action by faith in Him, **moves mountains.**

Begin your day in fellowship with the Lord and watch Him move the mountains out of your way as you journey through this day.

Ponder
DAY 6:
INTENTIONAL COMMITMENT

-Luke 6:12-13 (NLT)-12 "One day soon afterward Jesus went up on a mountain to pray, and he prayed to God all night.

-13 At daybreak he called together all of his disciples and chose twelve of them to be apostles. Here are their names:"

💭 - Think back to moments when you were with a group of friends or acquaintances and you needed to speak with one of them privately.

What did you do?

You probably asked the person to step away from the group with you to prevent distraction, and ensure privacy.

Jesus constantly communicated with the Father, often spending private intimate time in prayer on the mountain .

In His private prayer time, Jesus always sought the counsel of the Father and received guidance in all things—not taking matters into His own hands.

📓 - John 12:49-50 (NLT)-49 "I don't speak on my own authority. The Father who sent me has commanded me what to say and how to say it.

📓 - 50 And I know his commands lead to eternal life; so, I say whatever the Father tells me to say."

💭 - Any time can be prayer time. If you choose to pray during a business meeting silently, without changing your posture, hallelujah! However, it's really important to **make** time for alone-time with the Lord. Private time in prayer is the best way to receive whatever the Holy Spirit has for you, and for you to share your heart to the fullest.

Intimate time requires intentionality and commitment.

The Lord is intentional about being with you.

How about you? Begin your day by being intentional about being in prayer with the Lord.

DAY 7: MY JOURNAL

This week you learned intimate time requires intentionality and commitment. The Lord is intentional about being with you. Prayer is your heart talking to His heart and then His desires will become your desires.

Record what you learned during your intimate times with Him this week.

_____
_____
_____
_____
_____
_____
_____
_____
_____
_____
_____

Week 4
BREAD IS NECESSARY

My wife and I enjoy dining out. One of our top five places to dine is Romano's Macaroni Grill, specializing in Italian American cuisine. We love the warm inviting ambiance. The décor and the Italian matriarch kitchen setting add all the more to the dining experience. Once we're seated and given menus, the cameriere/cameriera (waiter/waitress) brings a loaf of **warm** rosemary peasant **bread** served with olive oil in a small shallow bowl and cracked pepper.

The bread is to die for; it's so good that we usually finish the bread before the meal arrives. Yes, you probably understand what I'm saying. The bread is the meal before the meal. In fact, we rarely have room for the main course and a takeout box is the norm. I'm certainly not disregarding the main course. I've never left Romano's Macaroni Grill unsatisfied, **but oh, my goodness the bread!**

The days Jesus walked the earth, bread was a staple of most dishes. In fact, bread and fish were the common meal. Today's culture hasn't varied too much. Think about today's fast-food restaurants like McDonald's and hamburgers 🍔.

What about Nathan's Famous hot dogs and Portillo's hot dogs?

We can't forget Pizza Hut and Domino's pizza.

How about Panera Bread, Subway, and Jersey Mike's?

Surely on this list, we must include our morning donuts!

How about birthday cakes and thanksgiving with bread stuffing.

Bread is everywhere and is still an important part of most meals.

Why?

> **Bread is filling.**
>
> **Bread is satisfying.**
>
> **Bread is sustenance.**
>
> **Bread is nutritional.**
>
> **Bread is necessary.**

Today, bread gets a bad rap, but bread supplies a significant portion of the nutrients required for growth, maintenance of health, and well-being. It is an excellent source of **protein, vitamins, minerals, fiber, and carbohydrates.**

*Did you know that Jesus is the **bread of life?***

Jesus supplies everything we need physically and spiritually.

Have you partaken of this bread?

Muse
DAY 1:
GOD PROVIDES

Matthew 14:17-21 (NLT-) 17 "But we have only five loaves of bread and two fish!" they answered.

-18 "Bring them here," he said.

-19 Then he told the people to sit down on the grass. Jesus took the five loaves and two fish, looked up toward heaven, and blessed them. Then, breaking the loaves into pieces, he gave the bread to the disciples, who distributed it to the people.

-20 They all ate as much as they wanted, and afterward, the disciples picked up twelve baskets of leftovers.

-21 About 5,000 men were fed that day, in addition to all the women and children!"

 - **Everything is possible with Jesus.**

He can make a way out of no way.

He can use **whatever you have** and do **miracles**.

He can use your $1 dollar bill and multiply it infinitely to provide the needs for a countless number of homeless and needy people all over the world.

The Holy Spirit indwells the believer; Thus, having the bread of life within to distribute Himself through you, and your God-given gifts to change the world.

We have absolutely no idea what He can do through each and every one of us, if we sincerely give Him even the smallest portion of our hearts. He truly desires to have our whole heart, but He will work with what we give Him to start. He will blow our minds.

Here's a little bit about me and how the Lord used my morsel-size faith to open my eyes to His love and provision.

2013 felt as if it was the beginning of the end for our family. At this time, our two oldest, Jordan and Justin, were living on their own. My wife Tavia, and our two youngest, Savannah entering high school, and Jasper, eighth grade were together. We were new residents of a wonderful neighborhood. Great right?

Well, being new residents came on the heels of the early stage of our financial hardship. We moved to this lovely neighborhood by force. My love for real estate investments took a terrible turn. We owned several rental properties out of state. Seemingly out of nowhere, some of our rental properties needed major repairs all at the same time. We found ourselves pouring money into the properties, hand over fist.

I began to use my income to support the rentals, neglecting my own mortgage. **This was poor money management.**

Before long, we were four months behind in our mortgage and we weren't able to work anything out with the mortgage company at that time.

You can probably imagine our credit took a major hit. It was so bad, that we didn't believe any property management or landlord would rent to us, but God supplies.

My wife and I were constantly in prayer, **crying out to the Lord** to carry us through this nightmare and to provide a home for us. We were out one day, driving around different neighborhoods searching for rental signs in the front yards.

We spotted a home at the end of a cul-de-sac, with a **for lease** sign in the front yard. We parked and started walking towards the front door which was slightly open. We could hear men working on the inside, so we rang the doorbell and one of the men told us to come in.

As we entered, the homeowner stepped out of another room. We asked if we could take a look around and she agreed. After touring the home, the owner explained that she hadn't advertised the home at that point because she was having the home painted, etc.

"I just placed the sign in the front yard today. You two are the first to respond," she told us.

My wife and I expressed our interest in the home and she said she would consider it.

She took down our name and number and said, "I will call you in a couple of days with my decision."

True to her word, she called, and she was willing to accept us, but she required us to complete a credit application. She was a friend of a property manager/realtor.

We completed the credit application but were extremely concerned because our credit had hit **rock bottom.**

We nervously waited for the report, remaining in constant prayer. Two days later, the property manager contacted us and informed us that our credit wasn't the greatest, but the homeowner had a good feeling about us and accepted us as her tenants. The next day, we completed the lease agreement and praised the Lord like never before!

Not only did the Lord Jesus provide, but this house was much larger than our previous home and the backyard of our new residence was just across the street from the middle school my son attended. **Hallelujah!**

The Lord always supplies.

No matter what your need is today, take the time to share that need with your loving heavenly Father. He loves to supply for the needs of His children.

Muse
DAY 2: NEEDS NOT GREEDS

- Exodus 16:4 (NLT) - "Then the LORD said to Moses, 'Look, I'm going to rain down food from heaven for you. Each day the people can go out and pick up as much food as they need for that day. I will test them in this to see whether or not they will follow my instructions.'"

💭 - After the Lord God rescued the nation of Israel from Egyptian oppression, the Israelites became very hungry during their journey to the land of promise. The Lord promised He would never abandon nor forsake His children and He is faithful to His word.

The Lord **miraculously** provided food for the Israelites daily. This food was a type of bread called "manna" which is Hebrew meaning "what is it?". The Israelites had no idea what it was. Manna was a flaky substance, white like Coriander seed and tasted like honey wafers.

Every morning after the dew evaporated, manna blanketed the ground. Each morning each household was to gather as much as they **needed** for that day. Any family that gathered more than they needed discovered that the excess turned to maggots with a terrible odor.

The journey to the land of promise, Canaan, should have taken just a few days, but due to their disobedience, the journey lasted forty years. The Lord remained faithful to His promise and provided manna every day for forty years.

You may ask–"What does this type of **bread** called manna have to do with me?"

Ask Yourself…

> *Do you have a roof over your head?*
> *Is there **any food** in your fridge or pantry?*
> *Do you have **any clothing**?*
> *Do you have some form of transportation?*
> *Are you able-bodied and employed?*

Most of these are basic needs, and owning a vehicle is a **bonus**.

The Lord promises to supply our **needs**, not our **greeds**.

Everything we have comes from the Lord, but isn't life more important than anything?

The Lord has given us life.

- Genesis 2:7 (NLT) 7 – "Then the LORD God formed the man from the dust of the ground. He breathed the breath of life into the man's nostrils, and the man became a living person."

💭 - Life is more than just existing. The Lord Jesus desires us to live an **abundant** life that only He can give. He provides physical food daily for our bodies, but to live the **abundant** kingdom life (which is true life), we must consume more than physical bread (food).

📕 - Deuteronomy 8:3 (NLT) – "Yes, he humbled you by letting you go hungry and then feeding you with manna, a food previously unknown to you and your ancestors. He did it to teach you that people do not live by bread alone; rather, we live by every word that comes from the mouth of the LORD."

Heavenly bread is necessary.

Before you begin your day, stop and thank your heavenly Father for the "manna" He has provided for you.

Muse
DAY 3:
COME! PARTAKE!

– John 6:32 (NLT)–Jesus said, "I tell you the truth, Moses didn't give you bread from heaven. My Father did. And now he offers you the true bread from heaven."

💭 - Shortly after Jesus performed the miracle of the feeding of the **5,000 men** (not including women and children which most likely totaled 15,000 or more); many who were fed, began to follow Jesus. Jesus realized their motivation to follow Him, wasn't because they wanted Him.

📖 - John 6:26 (NLT)–Jesus replied, "I tell you the truth, you want to be with me because I fed you, not because you understood the miraculous signs."

💭 - The crowd wanted to perform signs like Jesus and wanted to see Him perform more miracles as well.

- John 6:28-30 (NLT)–They replied, "We want to perform God's works, too. What should we do?"

- 29 Jesus told them, "This is the only work God wants from you: Believe in the one he has sent."

- 30 They answered, "Show us a miraculous sign if you want us to believe in you. What can you do?"

- Jesus didn't come down from heaven to be a genie. He came because He is the true bread of life. He came to give to all who will believe in Him a purposeful, meaningful, peace-filled, and joy-filled life here on earth. Most important, He came to bring **eternal life** to all who will receive Him. Jesus is the satisfying heavenly bread everyone needs to navigate through their lives.

>Jesus is more than able to solve the difficulties of life.
>Jesus is the answer to all of life's questions.
>There's nothing Jesus can't do.

Ask Yourself…

*Do you know people suffering from some ailment or terminal illness who want the **healing**, but **not** Jesus?*

*Do you know others who are experiencing financial disaster and would love to receive a **financial blessing**, but **not** receive Jesus?*

*How about the marriages that are on the brink of divorce and need to see the Lord's **saving hand**, but do **not** have Jesus in their lives?*

*Do you know of anyone in need of a job/career opportunity or advancement, but are **not** willing to allow Jesus to bring them into this abundant life?*

Have you shared the wonderful news with those; that Jesus is more than able to solve the difficulties of life if they would just come and partake?

The Holy Spirit who dwells within the believer, teaches and brings understanding to those who desire to **know this abundantly life-giving bread.**

Won't you come and partake of His manna today and share what you have learned with those all around you who need to learn what you have learned about the bread of life?

Muse
DAY 4:
THE TRUE BREAD OF GOD IS ALL YOU NEED

- John 6:33 (NLT) – "The true bread of God is the one who comes down from heaven and gives life to the world."

- In 2011, my wife Tavia, gave her heart and life to Jesus. Prior to 2011, Tavia and her parents' (Melvin and Joyce) faith was rooted in the belief system of the Jehovah's Witness, albeit not active. As Tavia continued her new journey with Christ, she deeply desired to share the goodness of the Lord Jesus with her parents. Tavia wanted her parents to experience the same love and joy of the Lord that was being poured into her heart. Once a week, Tavia would invite her parents to Sunday church service––to no avail. After several invitations, Tavia's mother, Joyce, accepted.

I vividly recall the day Joyce attended. As Joyce entered the sanctuary, I noticed her countenance was down. She appeared to be on the **precipice** of a nervous breakdown. Joyce was so broken, and struggled to walk. One of the ushers, a sweet woman with a tender heart, greeted and gently held Joyce's hand and escorted her to her seat. The usher didn't seat Joyce with the family, but seated Joyce near her usher area to keep a close eye on her.

Throughout the church service, this amazing usher comforted Joyce. The pastor delivered the word of God with so much love and passion, you can feel the presence of the Holy Spirit moving through the hearts of the congregation. Immediately after the service ended, we rushed over to where Joyce was seated.

We asked – "Are you okay?"

She stood, smiled, and said, "l am fine, I feel so much better."

At that moment, the usher approached and asked Joyce, "How are you doing?"

Joyce answered, "I feel so much better, and thank you for everything."

The two embraced. That Sunday was a new beginning for Joyce. She attended church regularly and Tavia's dad Melvin became a regular parishioner as well. Jesus, the bread of life, moves the heart and feeds and nourishes the soul. He brings life to your spirit.

The true bread of God heals the soul.

The true bread of God is all you need.

Think of someone you know who needs to experience this true bread of life to heal their soul. Approach them today and invite them to attend church with you and let the Holy Spirit move on their heart.

Muse
DAY 5:
JESUS WILL FILL YOUR EMPTINESS

- John 6:35 (NLT)–Jesus replied, "I am the bread of life. Whoever comes to me will never be hungry again. Whoever believes in me will never be thirsty."

Maybe all is well with your finances and your stock portfolio is performing quite well . Your marriage is picture perfect and your family vacations are without bounds. Maybe you have traveled the world. Your career and or business is firing on all cylinders, yet you are still hungry for life, thirsty for more.

Is that you today?

Instead, maybe you are experiencing the other side of a picturesque life filled with doom and gloom, pain, and suffering.

Allow me to pick up my story where I left off, back in day 1 of week 4.

As we were settling into our new home, we continued trying to work through our financial difficulties. It seemed to be going well until the roller coaster of life began to roar and descend at a breakneck speed. My wife and her employer of eleven years decided to part ways which caught my wife totally off guard. Several months of applications and interviews brought **zero** results as she searched for employment. My faith began to wane, and worry set in, but Tavia pushed forward.

With one income, some tough decisions had to be made. The first and toughest decision was to voluntarily relinquish one of our vehicles which made trying to meet the needs of our family seem nearly impossible.

The second decision was to bring dining-out and all other entertainment outings to a screeching halt.

The spike-walled chamber was closing in fast. As The days grew dimmer, and our faith was being challenged, we pressed into the Lord more. Every Sunday after church service, our entire family and extended family would gather at our home to fellowship, enjoy brunch, and discuss how the Lord's message for the day touched us.

Our two oldest sons, Jordan and Justin, led by the Holy Spirit, held Bible studies in their home with a few of their friends once a week. Seeing this, the Lord placed it on our hearts to host a Bible study as well. We asked Jordan and Justin if they would facilitate a Bible study in our home, and they were more than happy to oblige.

Tavia and I were thrilled to host a Bible study in our home. Even though we faced days with very little in the fridge and pantry, we had the joy of the Lord and weren't going to allow our circumstances to redirect what the Lord was asking us to do. We believed the Lord Jesus would provide for our needs no matter what. Our desire to **know** the Lord continued to grow. This growth became evident in our desire to serve the Lord at church.

Tavia and I served as greeters and ushers. Savannah and Jasper served in the kid's ministry as assistants to the teachers for the second-grade boys and girls. The Lord opened a door for me to attend the School of Ministry.

All of these things were taking place as our entire family was ready to launch our first Bible study. Due to work schedules and school days, Friday evenings at 6:00 P.M. worked best for us. However, we were concerned about the turnout because Fridays are the beginning of weekend getaways, not to mention family dinner time, and dining out.

In the midst of all this, my wife applied for unemployment benefits. She was awarded benefits, although minimal, **we were so grateful**. The hand of the Lord was doing a work behind the scenes and before our eyes.

We finally launched our first Friday night Bible study. We invited our extended family, friends, a few church members, and some classmates from the School of Ministry. The Bible study was a success. The Lord made it possible for us to provide our guests with wonderful appetizers, refreshments, and coffee.

The Friday night Bible study began to grow. Some nights we had upwards of twenty guests. Our guests enjoyed every Bible study and looked forward to the next one. We were equally excited and joyfully looked forward to each Friday. As a result of what the Lord was doing, one of our guests launched his own Saturday morning Bible study.

Financially, things remained difficult, but we were all serving the Lord and hungry for more. We couldn't get enough of what He was doing in us and through us. Every square inch of our home was filled with joy regardless of our struggles.

My next-door neighbor, Greg was wonderful, always in good spirits, and seemed to be quite the family man. I enjoyed having a conversation with Greg. One day, he mentioned to me that he noticed our family leaving every Sunday morning at the same time and returning around the same time. Greg was usually in his front yard working on some family project or working on his car, so I wasn't surprised about his observation.

I shared with him our love of Jesus and where we attend church- Water of Life Community Church which was only 2 minutes away

Greg said, "Yes, I'm familiar with the Water of Life Community Church. As a matter of fact, I attended the church for a bit. The pastor is a really good teacher, I really like him."

I asked, "Are you currently attending?"

He answered, "No, we haven't attended church at all in quite some time. I've been doing my life without the Lord."

Greg then asked about our Friday night gatherings. He had no idea what was going on. I explained that it was a Bible study, how it operates, the freedom to participate or simply listen in, the freedom to share any of life's issues troubling your heart, the freedom to bring and share your favorite scripture or a scripture that may seem a bit confusing, and closing out the evening with amazing appetizers, refreshments, and fun-loving fellowship.

After giving him the rundown, I invited him and his family to join us. True to his word, he joined, but without his family.

That Friday night Bible study was **incredible.** The Spirit of the Lord moved powerfully through the Bible study, touching every heart. Greg was so moved, he opened his heart and shared the troubles he was experiencing in his family. One of our guests prayed over him and comforted him.

That following Sunday, Greg and his family attended Water of Life Community Church. Immediately after the service, Greg and his family approached the altar for prayer.

Jesus, the bread of life, was slowly revealing to me and my family His purpose for our lives.

His words are so true. Whoever comes to Him will not hunger for the things of this world which will leave you filled with **emptiness.**

Jesus, the true bread of life.

Jesus satisfies the soul.

Ask Yourself…

*- Has there ever been a time in your life when life seemed to have absolutely **no** meaning, **no** purpose?*

Did life feel empty?

Why don't you turn to the true bread of life this morning before you begin your day and let Him satisfy your soul?

Muse
DAY 6:
JESUS IS THE ANSWER 4 LIFE

- John 6:48 (NLT) – "Yes, I am the bread of life!"

- I believe it's safe to say that we've all experienced a day when we've traveled back and forth across town to fulfill our shopping needs: supermarket, clothing store, automotive care, and most definitely a quick fast-food pick-up.

At the end of a day like that, you were exhausted and probably said to yourself, "Well, I got it all done."

The crazy running around town shopping days, is changing year by year. Wherever you live, there's probably a superstore that has just about everything you need, including automotive service and some sort of fast-food restaurant. Their goal is to be the sole source of your shopping experience and meet the **needs** of everyone.

In our scripture, Jesus is saying that He is **everything** everyone needs. Jesus is the **only** way to salvation and eternal life.

Jesus is the provider of life.
Jesus is the protector of life.
Jesus is the pleasure of life.
Jesus is the promise of life.

- John 14:6 (NLT)–Jesus told him, "I am the way, the truth, and the life. No one can come to the Father except through me."

- Here's an old cliche: "**You are what you eat.**"

If we often feast on junk food, the chances are very good our health will suffer. If we concentrate on a healthy diet, the chances of living a healthy life increase.

When we feed on and digest the bread of life, we are **promised** a spiritually healthy and physically sound life. Jesus is the **answer 4 life** and in Him, everyone will find their purpose in life.

You may have a wonderful career, a beautiful home, and a lifestyle that many can only dream of, but that's not your purpose. Partake of the Lord, taste, and see that He is good.

- Psalm 34:8 (NLT) – "Taste and see that the LORD is good. Oh, the joys of those who take refuge in him!"

Seek Him in all things, listen to the gentle voice of His Holy Spirit, then you will begin to see your purpose for living.

DAY 7: MY JOURNAL

Jesus is more than able to solve the difficulties of life.
Jesus is the answer to all of life's questions.
There's nothing Jesus can't do.
Jesus is the provider of life.
Jesus is the protector of life.
Jesus is the pleasure of life.
Jesus is the promise of life.

AS YOU CONCLUDE THIS WEEK, SHARE IN YOUR JOURNAL YOUR HOPES OF REALIZING THE PURPOSE GOD HAS GIVEN TO YOUR LIFE.

_____
_____
_____
_____
_____
_____
_____
_____
_____

Ruminate
DAY 29: CONCLUSION

As you conclude this 30-day journey from pressure to purpose, use these last two days to bring all that you have learned about God's plan and purpose for your life together in your final entries to your journal.

What week touched your heart the most?

Why?

_____

_____

_____

_____

_____

_____

_____

_____

Ruminate
DAY 30

IN YOUR SUMMARY OF THIS READING, SHARE HOW THIS DEVOTIONAL SPOKE TO YOUR HEART AND HOW YOU WILL NOW APPLY IT TO YOUR WALK WITH CHRIST.

INVITATION

If you have not accepted Jesus as your Lord and savior, I want to encourage you to make this decision, right now, at this moment.

This will be the best decision you will ever make.

Just repeat this short prayer out loud. You can do this privately, in your closet, in your car, wherever you choose.

"Lord Jesus, I know that I am a sinner and that I need you. Please forgive me for all I have done wrong. Please come into my life and begin to lead me. I pray this as sincerely as I know how. Amen."

If you repeated this prayer and meant it from the bottom of your heart, you are instantly a child of God.

Heaven and eternal life are yours and it's guaranteed!

A NOTE FROM THE AUTHOR

For many years, my all-time favorite movie was "Wall Street." There's a famous line in the movie where the star says, "Greed is good ." I truly believed that "greed was good" and applied that to my life. I lived it, I loved it.

The things of this world are temporal; the soul of a man is eternal. Our investment, while on this earth, should be in the things of the kingdom of God which are eternal.

The road to eternal destruction is broad, and many travel it, but the road to eternal life is narrow and few find it. Allow the wisdom of the spirit of the Lord to guide you down the road of right living; there will be difficulties, but the grace of the Lord is rewarding and all you need.

Choosing Jesus as the Lord of my life is the best choice I ever made, and I'm certain it'll be the best decision you will ever make. I still have a long way to go, but my faith is in Him alone. I pray you have made that choice now as well. – Dervon Dunagan

ABOUT THE AUTHOR

Born in 1965, raised in Pasadena, California. I'm a husband to an amazing wife of thirty-four years, and a father to four incredible children; three sons and one daughter–all adults. I'm also an elated grandparent of two.

I was a proud letter carrier with the United States Postal Service for thirty-six years; now a retiree as of September 30, 2021.

At the age of fourteen, in 1979, I accepted Jesus as my Lord and savior, however, in all of my teenage years and most of my adult years, my life was anything but Christ-like. As a husband and father, I learned so much about life, and about myself. Along the way, I made **many** mistakes as a husband and father which I deeply regret.

I experienced trials, triumphs, setbacks, and heartaches, but what I didn't realize, God was doing a work in me. In all of my endeavors: licensed real estate agent, loan agent, stock market investments, multiple rental properties, and an assistant coach for youth sports, there was a craving that I couldn't satisfy. There was something missing, a void, emptiness that I couldn't fill.

In 2010, I recommitted my life to Christ full throttle; Jesus filled that void, that emptiness. I dove headfirst into God's Word (the Bible) daily, listening to Christian radio sermons to and from work, hosting small group Bible study weekly, attending and graduating the school of ministry in 2017, and partnering with a dear friend to launch a men's ZOOM Bible study in the midst of the 2020 Coronavirus pandemic.

The insatiable desire for the things of this world and all it offered; God used that burning desire and transformed it into a **hunger** to know Him and please Him.

This hunger within me is none other than the Holy Spirit of the Lord, empowering me to author this book.

All the thanks and glory to God, for the trials, travails, and triumphs in my life. I'm still a work in progress, God is not finished with me. I'm **not** where I want to be, but I'm not where I **used** to be.

I praise the Lord for the peaks and valleys of life; life is a journey, and each day is a journey **within** the journey.

Each day has meaning and purpose, so the Lord has placed in my heart this yearning to share the good news about Him to every soul that He brings into my life--extended family, friends, colleagues, and neighbors.

My prayer for you is that you will experience your journey with Christ and receive all of the joy and fulfillment it will bring.

May God richly bless you in all that you do.

Dervon Dunagan

Contact info:

https://facebook.com/Answers-4-Life-1047415948691514/
http://linkedin.com/in/dervon-dunagan-25106611
Twitter: DervonD1

Keep in touch with this link for future books by Dervon.